500 Riddles for Clever Kids

BRAIN TEASERS FOR THE WHOLE FAMILY

PETER PAUPER PRESS, INC.
Rye Brook, New York

PETER PAUPER PRESS

In 1928, at the age of twenty-two, Peter Beilenson began printing books on a small press in the basement of his parents' home in Larchmont, New York. Peter—and later, his wife, Edna—sought to create fine books that sold at "prices even a pauper could afford."

Today, still family owned and operated, Peter Pauper Press continues to honor our founders' legacy of quality, value, and fun for big kids and small kids alike.

Designed by Heather Zschock
Images used under license from Shutterstock.com

Copyright © 2022 Peter Pauper Press, Inc.
3 International Drive
Rye Brook, NY 10573 USA
All rights reserved
ISBN 978-1-4413-3952-2
Printed in China

Published in the United Kingdom and Europe by
Peter Pauper Press, Inc. c/o White Pebble International
Units 2-3, Spring Business Park
Stanbridge Road
Havant, Hampshire PO9 2GJ, UK

7 6 5 4 3 2

Visit us at www.peterpauper.com

Contents

Hey there, Super Sleuths!

Did you know that your mind is a muscle? Well, brain teasers can help you stretch it! With this collection of mind games, you can work out your brain, think in new ways, and most importantly, have fun!

In this book, you'll see many different kinds of riddles. Some are short, some are long, some are funny, and some are real head-scratchers! But all require just a few key tips to crack them!

Riddle Tips for All (Soon-to-Be) Puzzle Masters:

- Think about wordplay—many riddles use metaphors and personification. Be on the lookout for words and phrases with multiple meanings!

- Don't settle on the obvious! Sometimes puzzles will try and lead you in the wrong direction.

- Relax! Riddles ask you to be your creative self and consider new possibilities, which is easiest when you're having fun.

So, whether you're puzzling alone or with friends, flip through this book and find a riddle for every occasion!

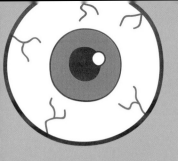

What Am I?

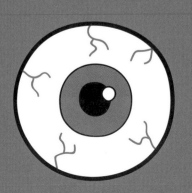

1. I speak without a mouth and hear without ears. I have no body, but appear with the wind. What am I?

2. I have cities, but no people. I have mountains, but no trees. I have water, but no fish. What am I?

3. I'm quick when I'm thin and slow when I'm fat. You measure my life in hours. The wind is my enemy. What am I?

4. I have hands but no arms, a face but no eyes, I can give you information but I can't tell you "hi." What am I?

5. I have a mouth but do not eat. I have a bank, but no money. I have a bed but do not sleep. I wave, but I have no hands. What am I?

6. Forward I'm heavy, backward I'm not. What am I?

7. When you need me, you throw me away. When you no longer need me, you bring me back. What am I?

8. If you throw me out a window,
you'll leave a grieving wife.
Bring me back, but through the door,
and you'll grant someone a new life.
What am I?

9. I travel all over the world, yet I stay in the
same spot. What am I?

10. I am an odd number, but if you take away a
single letter, I become even. What am I?

11. I have a tongue but no mouth.
I have feet but no legs. What am I?

12. You can find me in the woods.
The more you look for me,
the more you feel me.
When you find me, you throw me away.
What am I?

13. I have no wings but sport a tail,
and across the sky is where I sail.
I have no eyes, no ears, and no mouth.
I fly along from north to south.
What am I?

14.

I can fly, I can walk, and I can swim, but I don't get wet. What am I?

15. I'm not alive but I can die. What am I?

16. I belong to you, but others will always use me more. What am I?

17. I have a tail but no fur.
I have a head but no body.
What am I?

18. You take me from my home,
eat my flesh, drink my blood,
and throw away my skin. What am I?

19. I have branches, but no fruit, trunk,
or leaves. What am I?

20. I have the most stories of any building
in town, but I'm not the tallest.
What am I?

21. I fill a room, but I take up no space.
What am I?

22. In the form of a fork I hit the ground.
If you wait a moment, you hear my sound.
What am I?

23. I hold golden treasure but can be bought for change. What am I?

24. I can bring down the strongest people.
I am the enemy of flight.
No one can defy me.
What am I?

25. I am the gardener pulling weeds,
the leader making decrees,
the tailor sewing clothes,
the cook boiling greens.
What am I?

26. I travel high and low, but never move an inch.
What am I?

27. On invisible wings I fly.
If I am with my siblings, I start to cry.
Some pray for me, and others despise me.
Darkness follows wherever I go.
What am I?

28. I am filled with keys but can't open a lock. I'm concerned with time, but not with clocks. What am I?

29. I sometimes wear a leather coat, and take you to new worlds without a magic portal. What am I?

30. Better old than young. The healthier I am, the smaller I will be. What am I?

31. A curved stick and a straight twig splits the cattle's eye. What am I?

32. The foolish person wastes me, the average person spends me, and the wise person invests me. All will succumb to me. What am I?

33. Two bodies I have, though joined in one. The longer I stand, the faster I run. What am I?

34. Though I am tender, I'm not to be eaten, and though I'm mint fresh, your breath I won't sweeten. What am I?

35. You never see me, but I'm always there, and if I am gone, you surely will care. What am I?

36. I've got many teeth, but don't worry,
I won't bite. You may use me in the morning,
and you may use me at night.
What am I?

37. I begin with "e" but only contain one letter.
What am I?

38. I am made with six letters,
but if you remove one, twelve remain.
What am I?

39. You see me once in June, twice in November,
and never in May. What am I?

40. If you drop me I'm sure to crack, but give
me a smile and I'll always smile back.
What am I?

41. The person who makes me has no need
of me; the person who buys me has
no use for me; the person who uses
me does not know I'm there. What am I?

42. I have pointed fangs and a strong, set jaw.
Despite my might, I am at your beck and call.
What am I?

43. I am not a goat, but I have horns. I am not a donkey, but I carry a load. I am not wealthy, but wherever I go, I leave silver behind. What am I?

44. I have eyes but cannot see. I live in the dark until you need me. What am I?

45. I can be cracked, and I can be made.
I can be told, and I can be played.
I'm loved by some, and hated by others;
you think that I'm one way,
but then I'm another!
What am I?

46. When you don't know what I am, I am something. When you know what I am, I am nothing. What am I?

47. I help you from your head to your toes.
The more I work, the smaller I grow.
What am I?

48. I am a seed with three letters in my name.
If you take away two, I'm still just the same.
What am I?

49. Use me for music and music will be made,
but just so you know, I cannot be played.
What am I?

50. People buy me to eat, but never eat me.
What am I?

51. I live in a little house all alone. It has no doors,
windows, or stairs, and if I want to leave,
I have to break down the wall.
What am I?

52. Two in a corner, and one in a room. None in a
house, but one in a shelter. What am I?

53. Sometimes I glitter and sometimes do not.
Sometimes I'm cold and sometimes I'm hot.
I'm always changing, though your eyes
cannot measure; concealed within me
are a great deal of treasures.
What am I?

54. I run circles around you. Hang out with me
too long, and you'll be burned, but stay away,
and you'll wish you were near me.
What am I?

When I am
young,
I am sweet.
When I am
middle-aged,
I am bitter.
When I am old,
I am worth
more than
ever.
What am I?

56. I come in many shapes and sizes. You can put me anywhere, but there's only one place I really fit in. What am I?

57. I have no eyes, or legs, or ears, but my kind have moved the earth for years. What am I?

58. I am taken from a mine, and shut up in a wooden case, from which I am never released, yet I am used by almost everybody. What am I?

59. I can't be bought, but can be stolen with a glance. I'm worthless to one, but priceless to two. What am I?

60. Turn me on my side and I am everything. Cut me in half and I am nothing. What am I?

61. Sometimes I'm short and sometimes I'm hot. When I am lost, you won't like me a lot. What am I?

62. No matter how much or how little you use me, you change me every month. What am I?

63. I am harder to catch the faster you run.
What am I?

64. They fill me up and you empty me
nearly every day; if you raise my arm,
I work the opposite way.
What am I?

65. First I am dry, then I am wet.
The longer I swim, the stronger I get.
What am I?

66. Grown in the darkness,
I shine with pale light;
hung on a necklace,
I'm sure to delight.
What am I?

67. I have a big mouth,
and I'm known to be loud.
I'm not a gossip,
but I will get involved in your messy business.
What am I?

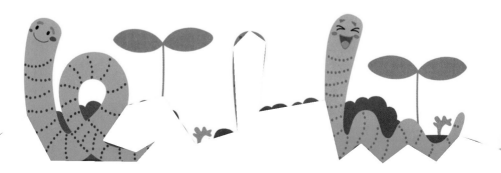

68. I have four wings but cannot fly. Still, you can find me in the sky. What am I?

69. Some try to hide from me, and some try to cheat, but in the end, we always will meet. What am I?

70. I weaken you for many hours a day, and show you strange visions while you are away. I take you at night, by day take you back. It doesn't hurt to have me, but you'll hurt from my lack. What am I?

71. I have no hands, but on your door I may knock, and if I do, you better open up.
What am I?

72. You don't want me when you have me, but if you must have me, you certainly don't want to lose me.
What am I?

73. I run all around a backyard, but never move. What am I?

74. I am made of water, but if you place me in water, I'll die. What am I?

75. I'm in a band but won't play music. Push me too hard, and I'll snap. What am I?

76. First you eat me, then you get eaten. What am I?

77. The more of me there is, the less you see. What am I?

78. I am lighter than what I am made of, and more of me is hidden than seen. What am I?

79. Without the first two letters, I'm an intelligent animal. Without the first three letters, I'm a subject in school. Finally, without the first four letters, I'm the letter "E." What am I?

80. I go around in circles, but always straight ahead. You'll never hear complaints from me, no matter where I'm led. What am I?

81. I have six faces but wear no makeup. I have twenty-one eyes but cannot see. What am I?

82. You bury me when I'm alive
and dig me up when I'm dead.
What am I?

83. You answer me, but I never ask you a question.
What am I?

84. I have two arms but fingers none.
I have two feet but cannot run.
I carry your objects safe and sound,
but I carry them best with my feet
off the ground.
What am I?

85. I stay where I am even when I go off. Although
you need me, when you hear me you scoff.
What am I?

86. We stand on lines. When together, it's a crime.
What are we?

87. I'm often talked of but never seen. You go to
sleep in search of me. Once you find me, I'm
still just as far away. What am I?

88. I live in the busiest part of the city. You can
stay for a while, but only if you feed me.
What am I?

89. I rest below the star above you and I;
a few stories below me is an empty space.
What am I?

90. I'm both the god of travelers and a rock in
space. I can name the temperature of any given
place. What am I?

91. I'm not a creature, but I have five fingers.
What am I?

92. Who makes moves while being seated?

93. I'm always between the ground and the sky,
and always far in the distance. If you try
to reach me, you will always be met with
resistance. What am I?

94. I turn once, and what is out will not get in.
I turn again, and what is in will not get out.
What am I?

95. I go through cities, I go through fields.
I never move, and never yield. What am I?

96. When I'm used, I'm useless. Once offered, soon
rejected. In desperation, I'm often expressed.
What am I?

97. I have four legs, but no hair. People use me for hours, but don't go anywhere. Without needing to be woken, I am always ready for work.
What am I?

98. I'm shorter than the rest, but when you're happy, you raise me up like I'm the best.
What am I?

99. Different lights will make me strange; into different sizes I will change.
What am I?

100. I have one eye and cannot see. I'm sharp but won't answer what you ask me.
What am I?

101. Spelled forward I'm something you do every day. Spelled backwards I'm something you hate. Add an "R" and I'm a part of you.
What am I?

102. Without a bridle or a saddle, across a thing I ride a-straddle. And those I ride, by help of me, though almost blind, are made to see.
What am I?

103. My thunder comes before the lightning.
My lightning comes before the clouds.
My rain dries all the land it touches.
What am I?

104. I have only two words but thousands of letters.
What am I?

105. I can take down steel but can't handle the sun.
What am I?

106. When you see me with wings I am tall
and quite slender. Take them away,
I am stronger than ever. What am I?

107. I have three feet, but cannot stand,
and have no arms to hold me up.
Even so, I'll always measure up.
What am I?

108. I only lie down once in my life—when I die.
What am I?

109. I'm full of holes but strong as steel.
What am I?

110. Each day, people from all over the world come and visit me, but never stay for long. Still, when they come to see me, they show me a part of themselves they rarely show to others. What am I?

111. I possess a ring of water and a tongue of wood. With walls of stone, long I have stood. What am I?

112. I am twice in perpetuity and always within sight. What am I?

113. I promise, I offend, I direct, and I fight. What am I?

114. I am a five-letter word. I sound the same when you remove my first letter. I sound the same when you remove my third letter. I sound the same when my last letter is removed. I sound the same when all three are removed. What word am I?

115. I fly all day long, but I never go anywhere. What am I?

116. I have thousands of wheels,
but move I do not. Call me
what I am, call me a lot.
What am I?

117. Big as a cake, deep as a cup, and even a river
cannot fill me up. What am I?

118. People love to hear me, my song floats
along a wing. But I'm a little strange,
for I must bow before I sing. What am I?

119. You have me today, and tomorrow you'll
have more. As time passes, I'm less easy to
store. I don't take up space, but I'm only
in one place. I am what you saw,
but not what you see. So, what am I?
Can you name me?

120. I have no wings, but will fly. I have many legs,
but will not use them. What am I?

121. As a whole, I am safe and secure. Behead me,
and I become a place of meeting. Behead me
again, and I am the partner of ready.
Restore me, and I am the domain of beasts.
What am I?

122. I'm so fast you can't see me, though everyone else can see right through me. I don't stop until the day you die. What am I?

123. I am white, black, and read all over. What am I?

124. I dig out small caves and store them in silver. I build bridges and crowns of bright metal. Everyone needs my help, but many are afraid to seek me. What am I?

125. Glittering points that downward thrust, sparkling spears that never rust. What are we?

126. I'm like a man, but not much for saying. I stand up straight, unless the wind's playing. I'm well-known and famous for lacking a brain, and I work day and night in the sunshine and rain. What am I?

127. I am you, but you're not me; I must be taken before you can see. What am I?

128. You cannot see me, but I can see you. To be more specific, I really see through. What am I?

129. Pronounced as one letter, and written in three, I'm found often in pairs if you're looking for me. I'm blue, I'm black, I'm brown, green, and gray; I'm read from both ends and the same either way.
What am I?

130. A hole leading in, a hole leading out, connecting a cavern that's slimy throughout. What am I?

131. You go into the woods to find me. You sit down to seek me. You bring me home when you can't locate me. What am I?

132. Put too much pressure on me, and I cry tears as red as blood, but my heart is made of stone. What am I?

133. I always go up when I am going down, heading up toward the sky and down toward the ground. I'm present and past, and always serve two; let's go for a ride, just me and you. What am I?

134.

I move without
wings between
silken strings.
When I leave, you
will find only these
strings behind.
I'm not loved by most,
though I often
help many,
and I never take
payment,
not even a penny.
What am I?

135. I can slash without a knife, I can dash without legs, I can pound with no hammer, I can star with no sky. What am I?

136. I've existed for millennia, but I'm never more than a month old. What am I?

137. You can find me in water, but I never get wet; I can be blonde, redheaded, brunette. I'm easy to find, if you're so inclined, but if you don't like what you see, you better not whine. What am I?

138. A hundred feet in the air, but my back is on the ground. What am I?

139. I am the third from a sparkle bright; I thrive throughout the day and night. Although it seems like just a blink, I've had millions of years to think. What am I?

140. The strangest creature you'll ever find: two eyes in the front and many behind. What am I?

141. I can be found on fingers, in toolboxes, and in snails. What am I?

142. Mouth without tooth, neck without head. What am I?

143. High born, my touch is gentle. Purest white is my lace. Silence is my kingdom. Green is the color of my death. What am I?

144. It's true I bring serenity,
and hang around the stars.
But yet I live in misery,
you'll find me behind bars.
With thieves and villains I consort,
in prison I'll be found.
But I would never go to court,
unless more than one is around.
What am I?

145. I can be flipped and broken, but I never move.
I can be closed and opened and sometimes removed. I am sealed by hands. What am I?

146. I have a heart that never beats.
I have a home but never sleep.
I can take one's house and build another,
and love to play games with all my brothers.
I am a king among fools.
Who am I?

147. You use a knife to slice my head and weep beside me when I am dead. What am I?

148. I am a silver river that divides into four streams. You use me nearly every day unless you're feeling green. What am I?

149. Flat as a coin, round as a ring, I have two to four eyes, but I can't see a thing. What am I?

150. The clouds are my parents,
and my children are the fruit of the land.
The earth is my resting place,
and my presence is the joy
and torment of man. What am I?

151. I can be long, or I can be short.
I can be grown, or I can be bought.
I can be painted, or left quite bare.
I can be round, or I can be square.
What am I?

152. I am a path between nature's
highest masses. Remove my first letter
and find a path where a city dweller passes.
What am I?

153. I say all that I hear to whoever's around. I'm not an animal, though I make animal sounds. I'll repeat what you say and right to your face, but only if my tail is in place. What am I?

154. When hearing me, men stamp their feet,
the children dance, the women weep.
The men will weep, the women dance,
the children stamp their feet and prance.
The men will dance, the children weep,
the women stamp all of their feet.
For these things I do to everyone,
to all who live under the sun.
What am I?

155. I'm full of holes but still hold water. What am I?

156. I'm often white, and used for cutting and grinding. When I'm damaged, humans either remove or fill me. Animals find me a useful tool. What am I?

157. There's more of me the more you take away. What am I?

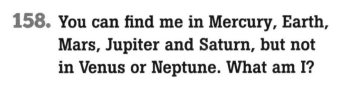

158. You can find me in Mercury, Earth, Mars, Jupiter and Saturn, but not in Venus or Neptune. What am I?

159. I am beautiful up in the sky.
I am magic but I cannot fly.
I'm said to bring luck and also bring riches.
Those who find my end will be
granted their wishes.
What am I?

160. I have a beautiful hall lined with red velvet, surrounded by bone–white chairs, and in the center, someone dances and sings. What am I?

161. The more you take of me, the more you leave behind. What am I?

162. I am not alive, but I grow;
I don't have lungs, but I need air;
I need to be fed, but water kills me.
What am I?

163. I am always in front of you, but you can't see me. What am I?

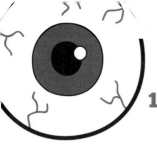

164. Take me out and scratch my head;
I am now black but once was red.
What am I?

165. From the beginning of eternity
to the end of time and space,
to the beginning of every end,
and the end of every place.
What am I?

166. If you say my name, I no longer exist.
What am I?

167. You peel my outside, cook my inside,
eat my outside, and throw away my inside.
What am I?

168. If I am behind, it means you'll have
work to make up in class. If I am down,
you may find yourself with an injury.
If I am out, you'll be left fighting
with a friend. What am I?

169. The longer I am, the stronger I become.
Only you may know my name.
If you forget me, you'll be sorry.
What am I?

170. I have roots that no one sees and stand much taller than all trees. Up I go, but never grow. What am I?

171. I have a neck and no head, two arms and no hands. What am I?

172. I am a word of six letters. My first three letters refer to an automobile; my last three letters refer to a household animal; my first four letters make a fish; my whole is found in a house. What am I?

173. I am a ball that can be rolled, but never bounced or thrown. What am I?

Answers: What Am I?

1. An echo
2. A map
3. A candle
4. A clock
5. A river
6. Ton
7. An anchor
8. The letter "N" (If you remove N from "window" you get "widow," and if you add N to "door" you get "donor.")
9. A stamp
10. Seven
11. Shoes
12. A thorn
13. A kite
14. A bird's shadow
15. A battery
16. Your name
17. A coin
18. An orange
19. A bank
20. A library
21. Light
22. Lightning
23. An egg
24. Gravity
25. A job
26. Stairs
27. A cloud
28. A piano
29. A book
30. A wound
31. A bow and arrow
32. Time
33. An hourglass
34. Money
35. Oxygen
36. A comb
37. An envelope
38. Dozens

39. The letter "E"
40. A mirror
41. A coffin
42. A stapler
43. A snail
44. A potato
45. A joke
46. A riddle
47. Soap
48. Pea
49. Your voice
50. Silverware
51. A baby chick in an egg
52. The letter "R"
53. A rock
54. The sun
55. Wine
56. A puzzle piece
57. An earthworm
58. Pencil lead
59. Love
60. The number 8
61. A temper
62. A calendar
63. Your breath
64. A mailbox
65. Tea
66. A pearl
67. A vacuum cleaner
68. A windmill
69. Death
70. Sleep
71. Opportunity
72. A lawsuit
73. A fence
74. An ice cube
75. A rubber band
76. A fishhook
77. Darkness
78. An iceberg
79. A grape
80. A wheel
81. A die
82. A plant
83. A telephone
84. A wheelbarrow
85. An alarm clock
86. Crows. A group of crows is called a murder.
87. Tomorrow
88. A parking meter

89. The number 8 (look at your keyboard)
90. Mercury
91. A glove
92. A chess player
93. The horizon
94. A key
95. A road
96. An excuse
97. A desk
98. A thumb
99. The pupil of an eye
100. A needle
101. Live
102. Eyeglasses
103. A volcano
104. The Post Office
105. Ice
106. A crane
107. A yardstick
108. A tree
109. A chain
110. A toilet
111. A castle
112. The letter "T"
113. A hand
114. Empty
115. A flag
116. A parking lot
117. A kitchen strainer
118. A violin
119. Memory
120. A caterpillar
121. A stable
122. The blink of an eye
123. A newspaper
124. A dentist
125. Icicles
126. A scarecrow
127. Your picture
128. An X-ray
129. An eye
130. A nose
131. A splinter
132. A cherry
133. A seesaw
134. A spider
135. A keyboard
136. The moon
137. A reflection
138. A centipede
139. Earth
140. A peacock

141. Nails
142. A bottle
143. Snow
144. The letter "S"
145. A deal
146. The King of Hearts in a deck of cards
147. An onion
148. A fork
149. A button
150. Rain
151. Fingernails
152. A valley
153. A microphone
154. Music
155. A sponge
156. A tooth
157. A hole
158. The letter "R"
159. A rainbow
160. A mouth
161. Footsteps
162. Fire
163. The future
164. A match
165. The letter "E"
166. Silence
167. Corn
168. Fall
169. A password
170. A mountain
171. A shirt
172. A carpet
173. An eyeball

Short &
Sweet

1. A man pushes his car to a hotel and
    tells the owner he is bankrupt. Why?

2. What travels faster: heat or cold?

3. Imagine you're in a small room with
    no windows and a locked door.
    How do you get out?

4. What do the words job, polish,
    and herb have in common?

5. What breaks yet never falls,
    and what falls but never breaks?

6. A man went outside in the rain with
    no coat or umbrella, but not a single
    hair on his head got wet. Why?

7. A man has a bee in his hand.
    What is in his eye?

8. Five hundred begins it, five hundred ends it,
    five in the middle is seen. The first of all letters
    and the first of all numbers take the spaces
    between. Now put it together and you will
    discover the name of a once-famous king.
    What is his name?

9. We are all very little creatures;
   all five of us have different features.
   The first of us in a jar is seen;
   the next of us you'll find in tea.
   Another you may see in a bin,
   and then a fourth is boxed within.
   By the fifth you're nearly done;
   you can find it in a bun.
   What are we?

10. A criminal is condemned to death. He is
    given the choice between three rooms.
    The first room is full of raging fires. The
    second is full of assassins with loaded guns.
    The third is full of lions that haven't eaten in
    years. Which room should he choose?

11. Two fathers and their two sons go hunting in
    the woods. They each shoot a deer and bring it
    home. They don't lose any deer but only have
    three when they arrive. How is that possible?

12. There's a question you can never truthfully
    answer yes to. What is it?

13. Draw a line on a piece of paper.
    Without touching the line,
    how can you make it longer?

14. Who is bigger: Mr. Bigger, Mrs. Bigger, or the Biggers' baby?

15. How far can a rabbit run into the woods?

16. A horse walks a certain distance each day. Two of its legs go 30 miles a day, and the other two go nearly 31 miles. How is this possible?

17. What's at the head of an elephant and the tail of a squirrel?

18. It's raining at midnight, but the forecast says tomorrow and the next day will be clear. Will the weather be sunny in 48 hours?

19. Double it and multiply it by 4. Divide it by 8 and you'll have it once more. What number is it?

20. How many sides does a circle have?

21. Matt has a big family. He has 10 aunts, 10 uncles, and 30 cousins. Each of his cousins has an aunt who is not Matt's aunt. How is this possible?

22. What can go up a chimney down, but can't go down a chimney up?

23. Where in the world can today come before yesterday?

24. A railroad crossing without any cars. How can you spell that without any "R"s?

25. An elephant in Africa is called Sasha. An elephant in Asia is called Tasha. What do you call an elephant in Antarctica?

26. There is a one-story house in which everything is blue. The floors are blue, the walls are blue, the furniture is blue. What color are the stairs?

27. What gets wetter when drying?

28. There is a boat full of people,
but there isn't one single person on board.
How is that possible?

29. When asked to describe his children,
their father says, "They're all blonde but two,
all brunette but two, and all redheaded but
two." How many children does he have?

30. If it is 2,200 miles to America, 1,400 miles
to China, 1,800 miles to England, and
1,600 miles to Sweden, how far is Argentina?

31. A man dies of old age on his twenty-fifth
birthday. How is this possible?

32. What is cut on a table, but never eaten?

33. If two's company, and three's a
crowd, what are four and five?

34. What kind of coat is always
wet when you put it on?

35. What has four legs in the morning, two legs in the afternoon, and three legs in the evening?

36. Thirty-two white horses on a red hill. They champ, they stamp, and then they stand still. What are they?

37. What is something that dawns on you even when it shouldn't?

38. Two women drink poisoned iced tea. One woman drinks hers fast and lives. The other drinks hers slow and gets sick. How is this possible?

39. What must you first give me in order to keep it?

40. A girl has as many brothers as sisters, but each brother has only half as many brothers as sisters. How many brothers and sisters are there in the family?

41. What is 3/7 chicken, 2/3 cat, and 2/4 goat?

42. What word of five letters has one left when two are removed?

43. What word is pronounced the same if you take away all but one of the letters?

44. How can you spell "cow" in thirteen letters?

45. A dog can jump five feet high, but can't jump through a window that's three feet high. Why not?

46. What kind of room can you never enter?

47. What goes around the wood but never goes into the wood?

48. What stands on one leg with its heart in its head?

49. There is a green house. Inside the green house, there is a white house. Inside the white house, there is a red house. Inside the red house, there are many children. What is it?

50. What has a bottom at the top?

51. What wears a coat in the winter
and pants in the summer?

52. In a year, there are twelve months.
Seven months have thirty-one days.
How many months have twenty-eight days?

53. What word is right when pronounced wrong,
and wrong when pronounced right?

54. Before Mt. Everest was discovered,
what was the tallest mountain in the world?

55. What holds two people together while only
touching one of them?

56. What three letters can frighten a thief away?

57. What can be stolen, mistaken, or altered, but never leaves you your entire life?

58. He has married many women, but has never been married. Who is he?

59. What can be driven without wheels, and sliced while staying whole?

60. What rocks but does not roll?

61. A sundial has the fewest moving parts of any timepiece. Which timepiece has the most?

62. What are two things you can never eat for breakfast?

63. At night, they come without being called. By day, they are lost without being stolen. What are they?

64. Consider the following group of three. One is sitting down and will not get up. The second eats as much as possible but is always hungry. The third disappears soon after arriving. What are they?

65.

Walk on the living,
they don't even
mumble.
Walk on the
dead, they mutter
and grumble.
What are they?

66. What word contains 26 letters but
    only has three syllables?

67. What loses its head in the morning
    and gets it back at night?

68. The last man on Earth received a phone call.
    Who was the caller?

69. What is it that, given one, you'll have
    either two or none?

70. You enter a small room.
    The doors close.
    When they open again,
    you're in a different room.
    How is this possible?

71. What has ten letters and starts with gas?

72. They can be harbored, but few hold water.
    You can nurse them, but only by holding them
    against someone else. You can carry them,
    but not with your arms. You can bury them,
    but not in the earth. What are they?

73. Who can finish a book without finishing
    a sentence?

74. What becomes whiter the dirtier it gets?

75. A man wants to buy a used car. He finds one for five thousand dollars, and takes it home without paying a dime. How is this possible?

76. Only the maker knows the cost of its making. It's worthless if bought, but is often exchanged. Any can give one, noble or poor. When one is broken, pain is assured. What is it?

77. There's nothing inside it and it's light as a feather, yet ten men together cannot lift it. What is it?

78. The sun bakes them, the hand breaks them, the foot treads them, the mouth tastes them. What are they?

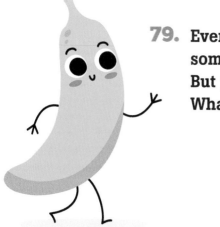

79. Everyone has some. You can lose some, and you can gain some. But you cannot live without it. What is it?

80. Never bought and never sold, but often valued more than gold. It is built, but not by stone, and when it's lost can't be regrown. What is it?

81. A time when they're green, a time when they're brown, but both times, they cause me to frown. But just in between, for a very short while, they're perfect and yellow and cause me to smile. What are they?

82. There is an ancient invention, still used in parts of the world today, that allows people to see through walls. What is it?

83. What has wheels and flies, but is not an aircraft?

84. Alive without breath, and colder than death. Never thirsty, always drinks; armored in mail that never clinks. What is it?

85. A boy left home running. He ran for a bit and then turned left, and then did the same twice more and arrived home, where two masked men were waiting for him. Who were they?

86. A cowgirl rode into town on Friday.
    She stayed for three days and rode back
    out on Friday. How is this possible?

87. What has eighteen legs and catches flies?

88. A man was only doing his job when
    his suit was torn. Why did he die just
    a few minutes later?

89. When may my coat pocket be empty,
    but still have something in it?

90. The 22nd and 24th presidents of the United States of America had the same parents, but were not brothers. How can this be true?

91. One is to three as three is to five and five
    is to four and four is the magic number.
    What is the pattern?

92. The day before two days after the day before
    tomorrow is Sunday. What day is it today?

93. How do you go from 98 to 72 using
    just one letter?

94. At the grocery store, an apple is one dollar, an avocado is two dollars, and a banana is one dollar and fifty cents. How much is a cucumber?

95. If you go to the movies and you're paying, is it cheaper to take one friend to the movies twice, or two friends to the movies at the same time?

96. A horse jumps over the king, knocking him out, but leaving no scratch on him. How is this possible?

97. On a local farm, there are three sheep, two dogs, a goat, and a farmer. How many feet are there?

98. On your bookshelf, one book is seventh from the left and sixth from the right. How many books are on the shelf?

99. Just two days ago, a man jumped through a window on the thirtieth story of a building without suffering any injuries, but it didn't make headlines or cause any alarm. Why?

100. If it takes one man three-and-a-half days to dig a hole, how long does it take two men to dig half a hole?

101. If 1=6, 2=36, 3=216, 4=1296, 5=7776, then what does 6 equal?

102. What is round on both ends and high in the middle?

103. Can a man legally marry his widow's sister?

104. Two sisters were playing tennis. They played five sets and each sister won three sets. How is this possible?

105. Jane is talking to her lawyer in jail. They're both very upset because the judge has refused to grant bail. At the end of the conversation, Jane is allowed to leave the jail. Why?

106. If there are eighteen pigeons on a line, and you shoot one, how many pigeons remain?

107. Is an old fifty-dollar bill worth more than a new one?

108. How can a man go ten days without sleep?

109. What do you get if you add six to thirty-six six times?

110. If it takes five microwaves five minutes to bake five potatoes, how long does it take one hundred microwaves to bake one hundred potatoes?

111. What starts with T, ends with T, and has T in it?

112. A man grabbed a woman's ring and pulled on it, then dropped it. How did this save her life?

113. If the date of the last Saturday of last month and the first Sunday of this month do not add up to 28, what month are you in?

114. How is it possible to always find what you are looking for in the last place you look?

115. If a wheel has one hundred spokes,
how many spaces are there between
the spokes?

116. What is the next letter in this sequence?
BCDFGH__

117. How high would you have to count before
you would use the letter "A" to spell
a whole number?

118. How can you take away two from five
and have four?

119. How do you spell candy in two letters?

120. There are four days which begin with
the letter T. Two of them are Tuesday and
Thursday. What are the other two?

121. Roommates Goldie and Flash are lying dead
on the floor inside their house. They died
from lack of water. There is a shattered glass
next to them. What happened?

122. Serena was born in the middle of December,
yet her birthday almost always falls on a hot,
sunny day. How is this possible?

123.

A person enters a room, presses a button, and loses 20 pounds within seconds. How is this possible?

124. A man who lives in a thirty-story building decides to jump out the window. He survives the fall with no injuries. How did this happen?

125. On a sunny afternoon, a child spotted a tiger in the distance. Instead of being fearful, she ran toward it excitedly. Why wasn't she afraid?

126. Three pieces of coal, a carrot, and a scarf are lying on the lawn. No one put them on the lawn, but no one wonders why they're there. What is the explanation?

127. Three people enter a room but only two walk out. The room is completely empty. Where is the third person?

128. A man fills a bag at the grocery store. He walks out of the store without paying, but no one stops him. Why?

129. What English word has three consecutive double letters?

130. Two men played chess all day. Later, they both celebrated, having each won every game. How is this possible?

131. A man is holding exactly $10.25 but only has one coin. How is this possible?

132. Max is outside of a shop. He can't read the signs, but he knows he needs to go in to make a purchase. Where is he?

133. Sitting at a four-legged table are one grandfather, two fathers, two sons, and a grandson. How many legs are under the table?

134. When is there a dash at twenty and a dot at sixty?

135. A rebus is a pictogram that represents a word, phrase, or saying. VA DERS means "space invaders." What phrase does the following rebus represent? O_ER_T_O_

136. Mrs. Wilson had thirteen children, and half of them were girls. How is this possible?

137. If 66=2, 88=4, 999=3, 7753=0, 555=0, 676=2, 832=2, then what does 2868 equal?

138. If you're ten feet away from a door and each move advances you half the distance to the door, how many moves does it take to reach the door?

139. You are given three positive numbers. Either adding or multiplying these numbers will get you the same answer. What are the numbers?

140. Two girls were born to the same parents, on the same day, at the same time, in the same month, and in the same year, but are not twins. How is this possible?

141. If a plane crashed on the border of Canada and the USA, where would the survivors be buried?

142. If an electric train is moving north at 50 mph and the winds are blowing west at 65 mph, which way does the smoke blow?

143. How can you drop a raw egg onto a concrete floor without cracking it?

144. A rooster sits at the top of a slanted roof. Which side are its eggs going to roll off on?

145. Jane walks into a diner and asks for a glass of water. The waiter instead loudly pops a balloon. Jane thanks the waiter and leaves. Why did she want the water, and why is she satisfied without it?

146. One knight, a ninja and a pirate were on a boat. The boat crashed, and the ninja and pirate both jumped off. Who drowned?

147. If there are three cups of sugar, and you take one away, how many do you have?

148. A man drives into a garage and sees three doors, each marked with a gem: a diamond, a ruby, and an emerald. Which door does he open first?

149. What is the coolest letter in the alphabet?

150. Matthew points to a boy and says, "He is the son of my grandma's only child." What is the boy's relationship to Matthew?

151. I am four times as old as my daughter. In twenty years, I will be twice as old as her. How old are we now?

152. What common English verb becomes its own past tense by rearranging its letters?

153. When asked how old he was, Jack replied, "In two years I will be twice as old as I was five years ago." How old is Jack now?

154. Decipher which of these words does not belong: Change, Brawl, Carrot, Proper, Sacred, Clover, Stone, Swing, Travel, Seventy.

155. How can you turn "new door" into one word?

156. There is a house. You enter it blind and leave it seeing. What is it?

157. A truck drove to a village and met five cars. How many vehicles were going to the village?

158. Which word/phrase is the odd one out?
CATWOMAN, DEUS EX MACHINA,
PARISHONER, SCUBA, PYROMANIA

159. What comes next in the sequence?
7, 8, 5, 5, 3, 4, 4, 6, _

160. What is the capital in France?

161. You are inside a square, glass room with all south-facing walls. You see a bear outside. What color is it?

162. Two scientists walk into a bar. One asks for H_2O. The other asks for H_2O too.
Which scientist dies?

163. A woman dropped an earring into her coffee, but it didn't get wet. How is this possible?

164. How do you fit ten horses into nine stalls?

165. The year is 2020. A girl tells her friend that she was born in 1964, but just celebrated her 16th birthday the previous month. She isn't lying, so how is this possible?

166. There are two monkeys on a tree, and one jumps off. Why does the other monkey jump too?

167. What five-letter word can you remove two letters from and still have the same meaning?

168. If a fella met a fella in a field of green, could a fella tell a fella what a fella means? How many "F"s in that formula?

169. You're riding a horse. There's an elephant in front of you, a tiger at your back, a cliff going up on one side, and a cliff going down on the other. How do you escape?

170. A is the brother of B. B is the brother of C. C is the mother of D. So what is D to A?

171. What are the next four letters in this sequence?
OTTFFSS

172. First, think of the color of the clouds.
Then, think of the color of snow.
Then, think of the color of a bright full moon.
Now, what do cows drink?

173. How is seven different from the rest of the numbers between one and ten?

174. Which word in the dictionary is always spelled incorrectly?

175. How can you physically stand behind your mother while she is standing behind you?

176. How can you throw a ball as hard as you can, only to have it come back to you, even if it doesn't bounce off anything?

177. Can you add one thing to 55,555 to make it equal 500?

178. Which is correct to say:
"The yolks of eggs are white,"
"The yolk of eggs are white," or
"The yolk of eggs is white"?

179. I have two newly minted coins.
Together, they equal thirty cents.
One isn't a nickel. What are the coins?

180. Find a number less than 100 that is
increased by one-fifth of its value when
the digits are reversed.

181. What four-letter word can be written forward,
backward, or upside down, and can still be
read from left to right?

182. What do the following words have in common: banana, revive, assess, dresser, potato, uneven?

183. You put a coin into an empty bottle and
put a cork in the neck. How can you get
the coin out without removing the cork
or breaking the bottle?

184. What does this rebus mean? I RIGHT I

185. My big piggy bank is a foot long and half a
foot tall. How many coins can I put in it until
the piggy bank is no longer empty?

186. During which month do people sleep the least?

187. Is the capital of Kansas pronounced Louis-ville or Lewee-ville?

188. What goes up but never comes down?

189. What can you hold in your left hand, but not in your right?

190. A sister tells her younger brother: "Two years ago, I was three times as old as you were. Three years from now, I will be twice as old as you." How old are they both now?

191. A truck is stuck under a bridge and the driver cannot get it out. A mechanic comes and easily gets the truck unstuck. How did she do it?

192. Which tire doesn't move when a car turns right?

193. When can you add two to eleven and get one as the correct answer?

194.

How much dirt is in a five-foot hole that is half a foot in diameter?

195. Can you guess the next word in this sequence?
Spot, stop, pots, opts...

196. A red house is made of red bricks.
A blue house is made of blue bricks.
A yellow house is made of yellow bricks.
What is a green house made of?

197. Why is the letter F like death?

198. Guess the next three letters in this series:
GTNTL

199. What is next in this sequence of numbers:
1, 11, 21, 1211, 111221, 312211

200. Using only addition, add eight 8s to get
to the number 1000.

201. The number 8,549,176,320 is unique.
What's so special about it?

202. A bat and a ball
cost $1.10. The bat costs
one dollar more than the
ball. How much does
the ball cost?

203. How many times can you subtract the number 2 from 50?

204. In California, you can't take a picture of a man with a wooden leg. Why not?

205. When is 99 more than 100?

206. A man meets a psychic. The psychic says, "I don't have many special powers, but I can predict the score of any football game before it begins." How can this be true?

207. You're running a marathon. Just before crossing the finish line, you pass the person in second place, and then two other runners pass you. In what place did you finish?

208. The day before yesterday I was 11, and next year I will be 14. When is my birthday?

209. What do an island and the letter "T" have in common?

210. The clerk at the butcher shop is six feet tall and wears size 10 shoes. What does he weigh?

211. A farmer has 25 sheep on his land. One day, a big storm hits and all but nine run away. How many sheep does the farmer have left?

212. Which is heavier: a pound of feathers, or a pound of steel?

213. Two children have the same parents and were born at the same hour on the same day during the same month. They are not twins. How can this be possible?

214. There five cookies in a bowl, and five children. You give each child a cookie, but one remains in the bowl. How is this possible?

215. A dog was tied to a five-foot-long rope and its food bowl was twenty feet away. How did the dog get to its food?

216.

Mr. and Mrs. Johnson have five sons, and each son has one sister. How many people are in the Johnson family?

217. A boy is ten years old in 2000. In 2005, he's five years old. How is this possible?

218. A taxi driver is going the opposite way down a one-way street. Several cars come up the street the right way, but the taxi driver doesn't hit them. How?

219. If you have one, you don't share it. If you share it, you don't have one. What is it?

220. A man shaves throughout the day, but at night, he still has a beard. How is this possible?

Answers:
Short & Sweet

1. He's playing Monopoly.

2. Heat. You can catch a cold!

3. Imagine a key.

4. They are pronounced differently when the first letter is capitalized.

5. Morning and night

6. He was bald.

7. Beauty (it's in the eye of the bee-holder)

8. David. In Roman numerals, D is 500, V is 5, and I is 1.

9. Vowels (j**a**r, t**e**a, b**i**n, b**o**xed, b**u**n)

10. The third room. The lions are dead.

11. There are only three men: a grandfather, his son, and his grandson.

12. "Are you sleeping?"

13. Draw a short line next to it.

14. The baby—he's just a little Bigger.

15. Halfway. After that, he's running out of the woods.

16. The horse operates a circular mill. The two outside legs travel farther than the inside ones.

17. "el"

18. No, because in 48 hours it will be midnight and dark.

19. Any number. If a number is doubled and then multiplied by 4, that's the same as being multiplied by 8.

20. Two. The inside and the outside.

21. The aunt is Matt's mother.
22. An umbrella
23. The dictionary
24. T-H-A-T
25. Lost.
26. There aren't any. It's a one-story house.
27. A towel
28. All the people on the boat are married.
29. Three. A blonde, a brunette, and a redhead.
30. 2,600 miles. Vowels are worth 400 miles and consonants are worth 200 miles.
31. He was born on a leap year.
32. A deck of cards
33. Nine
34. A coat of paint
35. A human (at different stages of life: a baby crawling, an adult on two legs, and in old age with a cane)
36. Teeth
37. The obvious
38. The poison is in the ice.
39. Your word
40. Four sisters and three brothers
41. Chicago
42. "Stone"
43. "Queue"
44. "SEE O DOUBLE YOU"
45. The window is closed.
46. A mushroom
47. The bark of a tree
48. A cabbage
49. A watermelon
50. Legs
51. A dog
52. All of them
53. "Wrong"
54. Mt. Everest
55. A wedding ring
56. I C U
57. Your identity
58. A priest
59. A golf ball
60. A rocking chair

61. An hourglass (with thousands of grains of sand)

62. Lunch and dinner

63. The stars

64. A stove, fire, and smoke

65. Leaves

66. "Alphabet"

67. A pillow

68. The last woman on Earth

69. A choice

70. You were in an elevator.

71. An automobile

72. Grudges

73. A prisoner

74. A blackboard

75. He doesn't use any dimes to pay for it.

76. A promise

77. A bubble

78. Grapes

79. Blood

80. Trust

81. Bananas

82. A window

83. A garbage truck

84. A fish

85. The catcher and the umpire

86. The horse's name was Friday.

87. A baseball team

88. He was an astronaut out in space.

89. When it has a hole.

90. They were the same man. Grover Cleveland served two terms as president of the United States, but the terms were not consecutive.

91. "One" has three letters, "three" has five letters, and "five" has four letters (and so does "four").

92. Saturday

93. Put an "x" between 9 and 8 (9x8=72)

94. One dollar and fifty cents (each vowel is worth fifty cents)

95. It's cheaper to take two friends at the same time (three tickets), because if you go with the same friend two separate times, you have to buy a total of four tickets.

96. The horse and king are chess pieces.

97. Two. The sheep and goat have hooves, and the dogs have paws. Only people have feet.

98. 12 books

99. He was a window-washer; he jumped into the building from the outside.

100. You can't dig half a hole.

101. 1 (1=6)

102. Ohio

103. No. If she is a widow, the man is dead.

104. They were partners playing doubles.

105. Jane is visiting her lawyer, who has been arrested.

106. None—they fly off at the sound of the shot.

107. Yes, fifty dollars is always worth more than one dollar!

108. He sleeps at night.

109. 42, 42, 42, 42, 42, 42

110. Still five minutes.

111. A teapot

112. They were skydiving, and she was unconscious. He pulled the ripcord, and the parachute opened.

113. Whatever month you're in when you're reading this.

114. Once you find what you're looking for, you stop looking.

115. One hundred. The space that comes after the hundredth spoke would be just before the first spoke.

116. J (it is a sequential list of consonants)

117. One thousand

118. Remove two letters from "five" and you're left with IV (four).

119. C and Y. C(and)y.

120. Today and Tomorrow

121. They're goldfish. Their tank cracked.

122. She lives in the Southern Hemisphere.

123. The room is an elevator. When an elevator accelerates downward, the person inside (temporarily) weighs less.

124. He lives on the first floor.

125. She was at the zoo.

126. A snowman was built in the yard, and then the snow melted, leaving these items behind.

127. The third person went out in a wheelchair.

128. It's a bag of trash he's taking to the dumpster.

129. "Bookkeeper"

130. They were playing separate games against different opponents.

131. He has a quarter and a ten-dollar bill.

132. An optometrist's shop.

133. 10 legs. There is a grandfather (a father), his son (both a father and a son), and his grandson (both a son and a grandson). This gives us six legs in addition to the table's four.

134. In Morse code.

135. The letters missing from "operation" spell out PAIN, so the meaning is "painless operation."

136. All of her children were girls.

137. 5. Each circle within a number is equivalent to one.

138. You'll never reach the door because each move will always get you only half the distance.

139. 1, 2, and 3

140. The girls are part of a set of triplets.

141. You don't bury survivors.

142. An electric train does not emit smoke.

143. Concrete floors are hard to crack.

144. Neither, roosters don't lay eggs.

145. She had the hiccups. The waiter scared them out of her.

146. The knight.

147. One (the one that you took).

148. His car door.

149. B. AC surrounds it.

150. He is Matthew's brother.

151. 40 and 10

152. "Eat" and "Ate"

153. He's 12.

154. Carrot (it's the only word that does not become another word when you remove the first and last letters).

155. Rearrange the letters—"new door" is an anagram for "one word."

156. A school

157. One (to meet the other cars meant they were going in the opposite direction).

158. Parishioner (It begins with a capital city, and the others end in a country: catwOMAN, deus ex maCHINA, PARISHioner, pyROMANIA, sCUBA)

159. 9. The sequence is the number of letters in the name of each month. "September" has 9 letters.

160. "F"

161. White. It's a polar bear at the North Pole (the only place where all the walls would face south).

162. The second. The bartender thought the second scientist asked for H_2O_2, which is hydrogen peroxide (deadly when ingested).

163. The earring was dropped into dry coffee grounds.

164. Like this: [t][e][n][h] [o][r][s][e][s]

165. She was born in room 1964 at the hospital.

166. Monkey see, monkey do.

167. Alone. Remove the "a" and "l" and you get "one."

168. There is only one "F" in "formula."

169. Wait for the carousel to stop and get off.

170. A is D's uncle.

171. ENTE (Each letter is the first letter of a spelled–out number, so One, Two, Three, etc. … Eight, Nine, Ten, Eleven).

172. Water

173. Seven has two syllables instead of one.

174. "Incorrectly"

175. You stand back-to-back with each other.

176. Throw the ball straight up into the air.

177. A minus sign. 555-55=500.

178. None. Egg yolks are yellow.

179. A quarter and a nickel

180. 45 (1/5 of 45 = 9, 9 + 45 = 54).

181. "NOON"

182. If you take the first letter of each word and place it at the end, it will spell the same word backward.

183. You push the cork all the way down the bottle and shake the coin out.

184. "Right between the eyes."

185. One! After this, the piggy bank is no longer empty.

186. February (there are fewer nights to sleep).

187. Neither. The capital is Topeka.

188. Your age

189. Your right elbow

190. 17 and 7

191. She let the air out of the tires.

192. A spare tire.

193. When you're looking at a clock.

194. None, holes are empty of dirt.

195. Tops (all of the words are anagrams of each other).

196. Glass

197. Because without it, life is a lie.

198. I, T, S (the first letter of every word in the sentence).

199. 13112221. Each set of numbers is a verbal representation of the sequence before it (one, one one, two ones, one two & one one, etc).

200. 888 + 88 + 8 + 8 + 8 = 1000

201. It's the only number including all of the digits arranged alphabetically.

202. Five cents

203. Once. Then you're subtracting 2 from 48.

204. A wooden leg can't take pictures.

205. When you're using a microwave.

206. The score of a football game before it begins is always 0 to 0.

207. Fourth place

208. December 31st (today is January 1st).

209. They're both in the middle of water.

210. Meat

211. Nine

212. They're both a pound, so they weigh the same.

213. They were born in different years.

214. The last child is given the bowl with the last cookie.

215. The rope wasn't tied to anything!

216. Eight. They have five sons and one daughter.

217. The boy was born in 2010 BCE. In 2000 BCE he's ten.

218. He was walking.

219. A secret

220. He's a barber.

Long
Form

1. A group of friends—Maria, Janice, and Lionel—
    meet up to play some music. Maria brings
    a guitar, Janice brings a flute, but Lionel
    doesn't have anything with him that Maria
    and Janice can see. They end up writing a
    wonderful song, thanks to Lionel's instrument.
    What did he bring?

2. The family matriarch was deciding how to
    split her will among her three grandchildren.
    She told each of them to bring her something
    small enough to fit in their pockets, but
    large enough to fill her bedroom. Whoever
    succeeded would inherit her wealth.
    The first grandchild brought some long
    scarves, but they only covered the floor.
    The second grandchild brought pockets full
    of sand, but they also only covered the floor.
    The third grandchild brought something that
    filled the room, and inherited everything.
    What did the third grandchild bring?

3. You're driving a bus. At the first stop, four
    people get on. At the second stop, one person
    gets off and another gets on. At the third stop,
    three more people get on. The bus is yellow
    and it's the middle of winter. What color is
    the bus driver's hair?

4. There are three houses. One is red, one is blue, and one is white. If the Red House is to the left of the house in the middle, and the Blue House is to the right of the house in the middle, where's the White House?

5. A farmer is traveling with a fox, a goose, and a bag of beans. During her journey, she comes across a river with a boat to cross it. The farmer can only fit one thing in the boat with her at a time. If left alone together, the fox will eat the goose, or the goose will eat the beans. How does the farmer get everything across the river safely?

6. A young boy is trapped at the bottom of the well. It's a thirty-foot climb to get out. Each day, the boy climbs up three feet, but because the walls are wet, he slips down two feet after. So, at the beginning of the first day, the boy has thirty feet to go, and at the beginning of the second day, he has twenty-nine feet to go, and so on. He has plenty of food and water, so he won't get hungry. How many days does it take the boy to climb out of the well?

7. Two boxers are in a match scheduled for twelve rounds. (Pure boxing only, no kicking allowed.) One of the boxers gets knocked out after only six rounds, yet no man throws a punch. How is this possible?

8. Amanda's mother had six children. The first was named Lala, the second was named Lele, the third was named Lili, the fourth was named Lolo, the fifth was named Lulu. What was the sixth child named?

9. You've planted sunflower seeds in your back garden. Every day, the number of flowers doubles. If it takes 52 days for the flowers to fill the garden, how many days would it take for them to fill half the garden?

10. A family lived in a big circular house. They had a maid, a butler, and a gardener. Once, the family went out of town for the night, and when they came back, they found all of their valuables stolen. They ask the maid, butler, and gardener what they were doing that night. The maid said she was dusting the corners, the butler said he was organizing the dining room, and the gardener said she was watering the plants. Who is lying and stole the valuables?

11.

A kid got in trouble and was sent to the principal's office. The principal said, "If you lie, I'll give you detention for two months. If you tell the truth, I'll suspend you for two months." What did the kid say to avoid both punishments?

12. A man wants to enter an exclusive party, but the only way to get in is to know the secret code, so he watches the bouncer to figure it out. A woman comes up and the bouncer says, "12." The woman replies, "6." The bouncer lets her in. Another woman comes up and the bouncer says, "6." The woman says "3" and the bouncer lets her in. The man is confident and goes up to the door. The bouncer says "14," and the man replies, "7." The bouncer kicks him out. What should the man have said instead?

13. There is a five-letter word and people eat it. If you remove the first letter, you won't need a coat. If you remove the first two letters, you must do it to live. Mix up the last three letters and it is a drink. What word is this?

14. You walk into a room and see a bed. On the bed, there are two dogs, seven cats, an ox, two seals, and a chicken. There are also birds flying around. How many legs are on the floor?

15. The first is in chocolate but not in lamb.
The second is in dates and also in yams.
The third is at tables primarily found.
This makes a soft friend who is often around.
What is it?

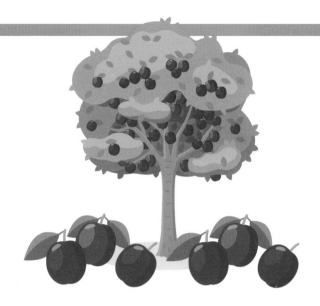

16. A woman owns a plum tree and supplies fruit all over town. One day, a shop owner calls and asks how much fruit the woman can sell. She knows her tree has fifteen branches. Each branch has another fifteen boughs, and each bough has four twigs. Each twig bears one piece of fruit, so how many pears can she sell?

17. You have eight white socks, eight blue socks, and eight black socks in your sock drawer. How many socks would you need to remove at random to definitely have a matching pair?

18. If you paint a blue house pink, it will become a pink house. If the stoplight changes from red to green, the light is green. If you throw a white shirt into the Red Sea, what will it become?

19. You stand in front of two doors. A guard stands in front of each. One door leads to death, and the other leads to paradise. The doors appear exactly the same. One guard always tells the truth, and the other always lies. Before you decide which door to go through, you may ask the guards one question. What question would you ask to make sure you choose the door to paradise?

20. There is a basket filled with hats. Three are purple and two are red. Three sisters, Gina, Tina, and Lina, each take a hat out of the basket and wear them without seeing their own hats or the hats the others picked out. They arrange themselves so that Gina can see Tina and Lina's hats, Tina can see Lina's hat, and Lina can't see anyone's hat. Gina is asked what color her hat is, and she says she doesn't know. Tina is also asked what color her hat is, and she says she doesn't know. Then, Lina is asked what color her hat is, and she does know. What color is her hat?

21. At low tide, ten rungs of a ship are above the water. The rungs are each five inches apart. Every fifteen minutes, the water rises five inches. After three hours, how many rungs are above the water?

22. You have a three-gallon bucket and a five-gallon bucket and an infinite amount of water. There are no other measuring tools. How do you fill the five-gallon bucket with four gallons of water exactly?

23. A family lives in an apartment building with an elevator. Every morning, the youngest son takes the elevator from the family's apartment on the tenth floor to the ground floor to go to school. In the afternoon when he comes home, he takes the elevator to the fifth floor, and takes the stairs up the remaining five flights. Why does he do this?

24. You are in a room that has three switches and a closed door. The switches control three lightbulbs on the other side of the door. Once you open the door, you cannot touch the switches again. How can you tell which switch is connected to each bulb?

25. In an art gallery, a man is looking at a beautiful painting of a young boy. He tells the other patrons, "Brothers and sisters I have none. But that boy's father is my father's son." Who is in the painting?

26. An old businessman must leave his fortune to one of his two sons. He gives them a proposition: both sons will race their horses, and whichever horse crosses the finish line last will inherit everything. During the race, the two sons ride as slow as possible, trying not to cross the finish line. Eventually, they ask their mother for advice. She tells them something, and then the two sons hop on the horses and race as fast as they can toward the finish line. What was their mother's advice?

27. Four cars came to a four-way stop, all coming from different directions. They can't figure out which car got there first, so they all go forward at the same time. However, none of the cars crash into each other. How is this possible?

28. A doctor and a bus driver are both in love with the same person, a woman named Angela. The bus driver had to go away on a weeklong trip. Before she left, she gave Angela seven apples. Why did she do this?

29. A local farm has only three types of animals: chickens, horses, and sheep. All of the animals but three are chickens, all but four are horses, and all but five are sheep. How many of each animal lives on the farm?

30. You have just landed on an alien planet that is similar to our world except in one crucial way. There are mirrors, but no reflections. There is pizza with cheese, but not pizza with anchovies. You can find coffee, but not tea. What is the one rule on this planet?

31. A woman shoots her husband, then she holds him underwater for over five minutes, and then finally, she hangs him. But later that day they both go out and enjoy a lovely dinner together. How is this possible?

32. Grandma Jones left half of her money to her son and half that amount to her granddaughter. She left a sixth to her nephew, and the remaining $1,000 to her cat. How much money did she leave altogether?

33. A small number of cards has been lost from a complete pack. If I deal among four people, three cards remain. If I deal among three people, two cards remain. If I deal among five people, two cards remain.
How many cards are there?

34. The king is trying to find a chef he can truly trust. Out of the candidates, James, Rachel, Paul, and Michael, he knows that two are always honest and that the other two always lie. Based on what each chef says, who are the liars?

James: **Neither Rachel nor Paul tells the truth.**

Rachel: **If Michael is a liar, then James is telling the truth.**

Paul: **If James is lying, then Michael is too.**

Michael: **What Paul said is a lie.**

35. Two men are in the desert. They both have backpacks on. One of the men is seriously injured, and the other is totally fine. The man who is fine has his backpack open, and the man who is injured has his backpack closed. What is in the backpack?

36. Marco lives in a place where half of the year has warm weather, and the other half is ice cold. He owns a lake, and in the center is a small island. He wants to build a cabin on the island and needs to get materials there. He doesn't have a boat, plane, or anything else to transport the materials. How does Marco bring the materials to the island?

37. The first two letters of this word signify a man. The first three letters of this word signify a woman. The first four letters of this word signify a great sandwich, and the entire word signifies a great woman. What is the word?

38. You have just broken into a bank and ask the teller for the code to the major safe. The teller says, "The code for the safe is different every day," and will not say anything else. You then open the safe. How do you do it?

39. This four-letter word is always done tomorrow. We're out of tea, the ultimate sorrow! Without the eye, you owe me some money. No sugar, no nectar, no sweetness, no honey. Four-letter word, if you happen to choose, whenever you win, it means that you lose. What is the word?

40.

You meet a famous sailor who poses the following question: "I have traveled the oceans far and wide. Once, two of my shipmates were standing on opposite sides of the ship. One was facing west and the other one east. However, they could each see the other clearly. How is this possible?"

41. Jennifer went skydiving in California, and as a result, saved her sick niece's life. However, her niece lived in New York, and hadn't seen her aunt in five years. How could this be true?

42. A man is planning a trip and is starting in Philadelphia and going to Tallahassee. He will stay one night, then go to Raleigh, then spend two nights in Atlanta before finally arriving in Florida. Where is he now?

43. What does a person love more than life, hate more than death or mortal strife; that which contented men desire; the poor have, and the rich require; the miser spends, the spendthrift saves, and all of us carry to our graves?

44. You're stuck in a room with no windows, doors, or vents to use to climb out. In the room with you is a light, a mirror, and a log of wood. How do you get out?

45. When Jenny was five years old, her mother hammered a nail into a tree in their yard to mark her height. Fifteen years later, Jenny returned to see how much higher the nail was. If the tree grew by five centimeters a year, how much higher would the nail be?

46. Two magicians were arguing. One boasted that she could hold her breath underwater for nearly six minutes. The other said that he could easily stay underwater for ten minutes with no scuba equipment. The first magician told him if that were true, she'd give him a hundred dollars on the spot. The second magician accepted the challenge and walked away with one hundred dollars. How did he do it?

47. One family wants to get through a pitch-black tunnel. The father can make it in one minute, the mother can make it in two minutes, the son can make it in four minutes, and the daughter can make it in five minutes. No more than two people can go through the tunnel at one time, moving at the speed of the slower one. They're all afraid of the dark, so someone needs to hold a flashlight at all times when they're crossing. Can they all make it to the other side if they have a single flashlight that only has twelve minutes' worth of power?

48. There was once a wicked witch. She stole the daughter of a baker and his wife and turned her into a rose bush, planting her among the many rose bushes in her garden. The baker and his wife begged to see their daughter once more, so the witch relented, and left the transformed daughter at her mother and father's house for one night before taking her back the following morning. That day, the baker decided to rescue his daughter. He snuck to the witch's garden, looked at all the identical rosebushes, and could immediately tell which one was his daughter. How did he know?

49. George, Helen, and Elena prefer drinking coffee. Bert, Gabe, and Jean prefer drinking tea. Using logic, can you tell if Elizabeth prefers coffee or tea?

50. A man is trapped in a room that contains only two exits. The first exit is constructed of magnifying glasses that fry anything under the sun. The second exit includes a fire-breathing dragon determined to kill. How does the man escape?

51. John and Jane are in a long-distance relationship, and John has just purchased a beautiful ring for Jane. He wants to mail the ring to her, but to make sure it isn't stolen, he wants to put a lock on the package. However, John has locks and Jane has locks but neither has a key to the other's locks. Without sending another letter/package, how can he get the ring to Jane and ensure it isn't stolen in the process?

52. A woman is sitting in her hotel room when someone knocks on the door. She opens it to find a man she's never seen before. He says, "I'm sorry, I made a mistake, and thought this was my room." He then walked away and got into an elevator, so the woman shut her door and called the front desk. What made the woman suspicious?

53. Ten candles are burning on a chandelier. A strong breeze blows through an open window, extinguishing three of them. Assuming the wind doesn't extinguish any more of the candles, how many are left at the end of the night?

54. Angela had a toothache. She went to the only dentists nearby, and was greeted by Dr. Canine and Dr. Molar, who were partners. Dr. Molar had lovely teeth, but Dr. Canine's looked like they needed quite a bit of work. With which doctor did Angela decide to book her appointment?

55. If you have a seven-minute hourglass and an eleven-minute hourglass, how can you boil an egg in exactly fifteen minutes?

56. You come across five beautiful chains, each made of four sterling silver links. You decide that you'd like to combine them all into a necklace of twenty links. You bring it to a jeweler, who tells you that the cost of making the necklace will be ten dollars for each link that needs to be broken and then resealed. What is the cheapest you could do this for?

57. After arriving at the center of a complex labyrinth, you come across five bags of diamonds, a perfectly accurate scale, and a stern chimera looking over you. All of the bags look identical, but the chimera tells you that one of the bags has false diamonds. All five bags are the same in every way, except the fake diamonds each weigh 1.1 grams, and the real diamonds only weigh 1 gram. The chimera tells you if you can determine which bag has the fake diamonds, you may take the four other bags home. However, you are only allowed to use the scale a single time. How do you determine which bag has the fake diamonds?

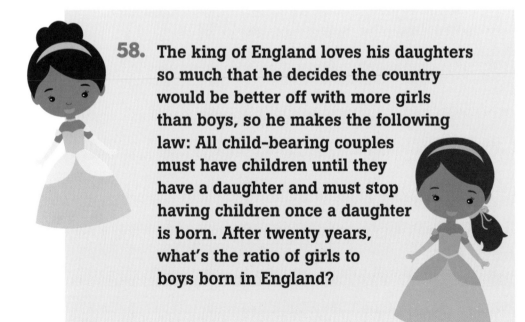

58. The king of England loves his daughters so much that he decides the country would be better off with more girls than boys, so he makes the following law: All child-bearing couples must have children until they have a daughter and must stop having children once a daughter is born. After twenty years, what's the ratio of girls to boys born in England?

59. Four friends—Abby, Lizzie, Stacey, and Eliza—all go to the same summer camp, where they can hike, zip-line, paint, and swim. Each friend has a different favorite activity. Abby's favorite activity isn't painting. Lizzie is afraid of heights. Stacey can't do her favorite activity without good boots. Eliza likes to look for shells when she's done. Who likes what?

60. Each of five neighborhood cats—Milo, Luna, Charlie, Leo, and Max—enjoys one of the following activities: getting its ears scratched, playing laser tag, taking a nap, eating catnip, or hiding under the couch. Leo is either playing laser tag or eating catnip. Neither Charlie nor Max is hiding under the couch. One of the cats whose name relates to the sky is getting its ears scratched. A cat whose name begins with M is playing laser tag. What is each cat doing?

61. Sally, May, June, Helga, and Pearl have their birthdays on consecutive days, all between Monday and Friday. Sally's birthday is as many days before Pearl's as May's is after Helga's. June is two days older than Helga. Pearl's birthday is on Thursday. Whose birthday is on each day?

62. Six brothers—Jack, John, James, Jason, Jerry, and Jax—decide to measure themselves. Jerry is taller than James but shorter than Jax. Jack is taller than John but shorter than James and Jerry. John is not the shortest. Can you put them in order of height from tallest to shortest?

63. Wednesday, Jane and Tom went to a restaurant to celebrate the completion of a big project at work. They ate filet mignon with roasted potatoes and shared an order of crème brûlée. However, at the end of the night, Jane and Tom got in an argument about who would pay for dinner. Eventually, Jane and Tom left without coming to an agreement, but the bill was still paid. Who paid for dinner?

64. After being mistakenly accused of a crime, you're put in a cell with a dirt floor and a single window. The window is too high to reach, and the only thing in the cell is a shovel. You have two days before the trial to escape, and you can't dig a tunnel out because it'll take longer than two days to complete it. How do you escape?

65. Janice went to the police and reported a stolen necklace. The detective went to her house and noticed that the window was broken with shards of glass on the lawn, the house was a mess, and there were dirty footprints on the carpet. The next day, Janice was arrested for fraud. Why?

66. A Swiss ship left its port on its way to new waters. The captain wanted to do some maintenance on the ship, so he took off his wedding ring and left it on his desk. When he returned just a few hours later, the ring was missing. He began interrogating his crew, narrowed it down to three suspects, and demanded alibis from each of them. The cook said, "I was in the kitchen making this evening's dinner." The medic said, "I was restocking the medicine cabinets from our last day at port." The first mate said, "I was on the mast correcting the flag, because someone hung it upside down." The captain could tell right away who stole his wedding ring. How?

67. A man eats dinner, watches some television, goes to his bedroom, turns off the lights, and goes to sleep for the night. The next morning, he wakes up. When he looks outside, he sees a horrifying catastrophe, and realizes it's all his fault. What happened?

68. On the first day of school, the English teacher's pet gerbil is stolen. She has her eye on four people at the school who might have stolen it—the history teacher, the gym teacher, the math teacher, and the principal—and asked each of them for an alibi. The history teacher said that he was hanging maps in his classroom. The gym teacher said she was running drills with her class. The math teacher said he was giving a midterm exam. The principal said she was meeting with parents. The English teacher immediately knew whose office to search for her gerbil. Who stole her gerbil, and how did she know?

69. A chemist is found dead in his lab. There is no evidence except a piece of paper lying next to his body. The paper is blank other than the names of five elements written on it: Nickel, Carbon, Oxygen, Lanthanum, Sulfur. Three people visited the chemist's lab that day— his uncle, Tony; his colleague, Nicolas; and his niece, Sandra. The murderer was soon arrested. Who was it?

70. A man, who thinks most art is a waste of time, runs into a museum and causes millions of dollars in damage. However, not only does he not get in trouble, the museum trustees all personally thank him later that day. Why?

71. Ten people sign up to test a new medicine with two different formulas. They are each brought into a room with a table that has a glass of water, one pink pill, and one green pill. One will give them a stomachache. Each is told to take one pill and leave the other. Some people take the pink pill and others take the green pill, but everyone still gets sick. How could this have happened?

72. One winter evening, a woman looked outside of her house and saw a man standing in the middle of her front yard. The next morning, she looked outside again, and he was still there. He stayed for several weeks, unmoving. Eventually he disappeared, but the woman never seemed to mind his presence anyway. Who was he?

73. A couple went on vacation for a month. They locked their house and gave a friendly neighbor a key to check in on the place while they were gone. When they returned, the husband was deeply upset to find that, due to a neighborhood power failure, his prized pocket watch was gone. He had hidden the pocket watch in what he considered to be a very safe place. He wasn't robbed, so how was the watch lost?

74. A man arrived at a dinner party and was about to hang up his coat when he heard the host shout, "No, Michael! You ruined it!" He could smell burnt lasagna. When he entered the living room, he saw the oven smoking. In the room he saw a security guard, an accountant, and a lawyer standing next to it. Who burnt dinner, and how did the man know who it was without having met any of them before?

75. A man buys a number of horses and takes them to his ranch. As he rides along, happy with his purchase and the good behavior of the horses, he counts them—fourteen, to be exact. He is perplexed, as he is sure he bought fifteen horses. Worried that one ran off, he dismounts and counts again—fifteen! He continues riding. About an hour later, he counts again and only finds fourteen. He climbs off the horse and counts again—fifteen! What is the explanation for this?

76. Four longtime friends sat down to play and played all night till the next day. They played for money, it was a chore, and everyone had a separate score. When it was time to check the books, a lot of cash is what each took. No one lost the slightest bit, so how would you explain this skit?

77. An old woman reported that she'd been walking in the town park when her brooch was stolen. The suspect had blonde hair and blue eyes, and carried a Prada bag. Police apprehended a woman who met this description. The suspect claimed she was relaxing in the park and saw a woman with brown hair and a Prada bag sneak up behind the old woman and steal her brooch. The police could tell the suspect was lying. How?

78. Julia was relaxing and watching TV when a rock crashed through her window. She looked out and saw three boys running away. She recognized them as the three Johnson brothers: Mark, Jason, and Neville. The next day, Julia found a note in her mailbox that read "?—He broke your window." Julia could tell right away who she needed to confront. Who threw the rock?

79. What eight-letter word can have a letter taken away and still make a word, take another letter away and still make a word, and continue to have letters taken away until there's only one letter left, and it makes a word every time?

80. A pet shop owner was selling a parrot and told his customers that the parrot could repeat everything it heard. A young girl bought the parrot and spoke to it every day for a month, but it never said a word. She tried to return it, but the pet shop owner wouldn't take the parrot back, saying he never lied about the bird. How can this be true?

81. There are forty people in an empty, square room. Each person can see the entire room and everyone in it without turning their head or moving in any way (aside from their eyes). Where can you place an apple so that everyone except one person can see it?

82. Jane is planning a hike through the wilderness to a faraway town. The hike will take Jane six days. A hiker can only carry enough food and water for four days, and people are not allowed to take animals into the woods to help them carry supplies. How can Jane make it to her destination?

83. Mary was in danger of failing her first college class and needed to ace her final in order to pass the course. She studied for weeks, and felt prepared, but on the day of the final, found the exam to be incredibly difficult. Her professor stated that anyone who took more than an hour to complete the exam would lose two letter grades. However, when the hour was up, Mary still wasn't done! She looked around, and saw that there were still plenty of students working, so she decided to risk it and just do the best she could. When she finally finished and went to turn in the paper, the professor said, "You were working past the one hour mark, so you're going down two grades." Mary indignantly asked her professor, "Do you know who I am?" The professor laughed. "No. Nice try, but that won't work on me." Mary turned in her exam, and later got it back with a perfect score. How?

84. A young man buys a collector's action figure for fifty dollars. After a month, the value of the action figure has increased to sixty dollars, and he decides to sell it. But a month after that, he regrets his decision, and buys it back for seventy dollars. Years later, he sells it for one hundred dollars. What is his total profit?

85. Jacob was making plum jam. He put all the plums in a pot and stirred them together. A little later, he remembered that he had to add one ounce of lemon juice for every two plums. How did he figure out how much lemon juice to use?

86. Three people check into a hotel room. The bill is thirty dollars, so they each pay ten. After they get to their hotel room, the concierge realizes that the bill should only have been twenty-five dollars. He gives five dollars to the bellhop and tells him to return the money to the guests. However, since five dollars can't be split evenly between three people, the bellhop decides to keep two dollars for himself and only gives the guests back three dollars. The guests, with a refund of one dollar each, have each paid nine dollars for a total cost of twenty-seven dollars, and the bellhop kept two dollars. That's $27+$2=$29. But if the guests originally paid thirty dollars, where's the other dollar?

87. Pick a number from one to ten. Multiply it by two, and then add ten. Divide it by two, then subtract the number you originally picked. What number do you need to pick to get a result of 5?

88. There is a barrel with no lid and some wine in it. One man says that the barrel is more than half full, while another argues that it is less than half full. Without removing any wine from the barrel or using any measuring implements, how can they determine who is right?

89. A man goes to the doctor with a stomachache. The doctor prescribes him seven pills and tells him to take them every half hour. How long do the pills last him?

90. A truck must cross a bridge exactly one mile long. The bridge can hold only one thousand pounds, which is exactly how much the truck weighs as it reaches the bridge. Halfway across the bridge, a bird lands on the truck. Does the bridge collapse?

91. A man goes into a store and buys a hot dog for three dollars, and hands the cashier a ten-dollar bill. She goes next door to get change and returns to give the man seven dollars. After the man leaves, the clerk from next door finds the hot dog seller and tells her she gave him a counterfeit bill. The man is long gone, so the hot dog seller gives the clerk a proper ten-dollar bill from the cash register. How much did she lose?

92. You are trapped in an empty, incredibly cold square room with no windows, no doors, and no heating devices. If you don't raise the temperature quickly, you'll freeze.
How do you get warm?

93. A man was driving a truck at eighty miles an hour. He didn't have his headlights on, and the moon wasn't out. However, he made it to the warehouse without an accident.
How is this possible?

94. Dr. Jonathan Johnson was an incredible surgeon in the late 1950s. He innovated new techniques and recorded a 90% operation success rate by the time he retired. However, most of his patients have died. Why does he still have such a good reputation?

95. A mathematician decides to give her son a gift for studying hard. She puts ten envelopes and one thousand dollars, all in one-dollar bills, on the table between them. She tells her son to put the money in the envelopes in such a way that no matter how much money she asks for, he can give her one or more of the envelopes with the exact amount of money requested. She tells him that he is not allowed to take out any extra bills from a different envelope

to reach the right amount. He thinks about this problem for a while, distributes the money into the ten envelopes, and receives the thousand dollars from his mother as a reward.
How did he do it?

96. There are thirty people at a party. Each person in attendance is very self-conscious, and only wants to shake hands with people who are shorter than them. Everyone at this party is of a different height. How many handshakes are made among the guests?

97. Find the country hidden in the following sentence: *Because we do not wish to overburden marketplaces in this hamlet, we will make sure the gardening shows are held on separate weekends of the month.*

98. You've just bought a cute rabbit from the local pet store. The shop owner tells you that the rabbit can breed once every month, and have six babies at a time. How many rabbits do you have after a year?

99. Jenna and Sarah went to the beach to play volleyball. They bet a dollar on each game they played. Jenna won three bets, and Sarah won five dollars. How many games did they play?

100. Two fruit farmers and aspiring poets are in an orchard, discussing rhymes. The first farmer says to the other, "What word rhymes with orange?" The second farmer thinks hard and says, "Nothing rhymes with orange." The first farmer thinks even harder and replies, "Actually, something rhymes with orange." Who is correct?

101. You are in a bathroom with no windows and a single door. You decide to take a bath and turn on the water, but when you shut the bathroom door, the handle breaks, locking you inside. You try to turn off the water, but the knob breaks, and water continues to pour out. How do you stop the bathroom from flooding?

102. You make a bet with your friend. She says she'll give you twenty dollars if you can drop a glass vase one hundred feet without it breaking. Its fall cannot be slowed, and its landing cannot be cushioned. How do you win the twenty dollars?

103. A music teacher has six children, and is expecting a seventh. Her six children are named Dorothy, Regina, Millie, Fannie, Sofia, and Laurie. What will she name her next child? Janey, Amanda, Tina, or Jack?

104. Timmy and Tommy were fighting. Their father was tired of it, so he put them on time-out by making them stand on the same piece of newspaper in such a way that they couldn't touch each other. How did he do this?

105. You have five children, and you have to get them all into a limousine. John and Jason can't sit next to each other because they fight, and Miranda refuses to sit next to the little kids, Jason and Macy. Neville insists on sitting with his brothers. There are five seats side by side. Miranda is the oldest and wants to go in first. In what order would you put the kids in the car so that there's no complaining?

106. A prize alpaca is on display at the county fair. Around its neck is a bucket with a sign: "Write Down the Exact Weight of This Alpaca and Win $100!" Expert alpaca breeders and veterinarians put their guesses in the bucket, but it's a clever ten-year-old who walks away with the $100. How did she win?

107. Matthew has invited his optometrist and her family over for dinner as thanks for her great service. After dinner, he washes the dishes, but when he looks down, he sees more glasses in the sink than there were when he began cleaning them. How is this possible?

1. He brought his voice.

2. A flashlight. When they turned it on, it filled the room with light.

3. Whatever color your hair is. You're driving the bus!

4. Washington, D.C.

5. The farmer brings the goose across the river first. Then the farmer brings either the fox or the beans across. Then she takes the goose back to the other side. Then the farmer brings the other item back (either the fox or the beans) and leaves the goose alone again. The fox and the beans are now on the other side of the river. The farmer returns and brings the goose across the river again.

6. He gets out on the morning of the twenty-eighth day.

7. The boxers are women.

8. Amanda.

9. 51 days.

10. The maid—there are no corners in the house.

11. "You'll give me detention for two months."

12. 8 (the number of letters in "fourteen").

13. Wheat.

14. Six. The bed has four legs, and you have two.

15. Cat (cho**c**olate, **d**ates, **t**ables).

16. None—it's a plum tree.

17. Four.

18. Wet. (The Red Sea isn't actually red.)

19. Which door would the other guard say opens to paradise?

20. Purple. If Gina doesn't know her hat color, then her sisters' hats cannot both be red, or else she'd know her hat is purple. When Tina also doesn't know her hat color, that means Lina's can't be red either, otherwise Tina would know her hat was purple based on Gina's answer.

21. Ten. When the water rises, the ship will rise too.

22. Fill the five-gallon bucket to the top. Pour it into the three-gallon bucket until it's full. Empty the three-gallon bucket, and then pour the remaining two gallons of water from the five-gallon bucket into the three-gallon bucket. Fill the five-gallon bucket to the top, and then use it to finish filling the three-gallon bucket. This will leave four gallons in the five-gallon bucket.

23. He can't reach the buttons higher than five.

24. Turn on the first two switches and leave them on for ten minutes. Once ten minutes have passed, turn off the first switch, and leave the second one on. Then, go through the door. The light that is on is connected to the second switch. The bulb that is warm is connected to the first. The bulb that is cold is connected to the third switch you never turned on.

25. His son.

26. The owner of the horse that crosses the finish line last will inherit everything. Their mother advised them to switch horses.

27. They all made right turns.

28. An apple a day keeps the doctor away.

29. The farm has three chickens, two horses, and one sheep.

30. There can only be words with double letters.

31. The woman is a photographer. She shot a picture on film, developed it, and hung it to dry.

32. $12,000. Use fractions to arrive at this answer ($1/2 + 1/4 + 1/6 = 11/12$, which means $1,000 is $1/12$ of the total inheritance).

33. 47 cards.

34. James and Paul are the liars.

35. A parachute.

36. He waits for the lake to freeze over during the colder months and carries the materials over.

37. "Heroine"

38. The teller has told you the code. It's always "different."

39. "Diet"

40. They were standing on opposite ends of the ship but facing each other.

41. Unfortunately, Jennifer didn't survive when skydiving, but donated her kidney to her niece.

42. Philadelphia. He hasn't left yet.

43. Nothing.

44. You turn on the light and look into the mirror. In the mirror, you see what you saw, so take the saw and cut the log in half. From there, two halves make a (w)hole and you can use that hole to climb out.

45. The nail would be at the same height as it was originally. Trees grow from their tops.

46. The second magician filled a glass of water and held it over his head for ten minutes.

47. First Mom and Dad cross the road—2 minutes. Dad returns—3 minutes. Both children cross—8 minutes. The mother returns—10 minutes. The mother and father both cross—12 minutes.

48. Because the rosebush was at the baker's home the previous night, and returned to the garden in the morning, she was the only plant without any dew.

49. Elizabeth prefers coffee. The letter "E" appears twice in her name, just as it does for those who prefer drinking coffee over tea.

50. He waits until the sun is down and runs through the first exit.

51. John puts a lock on the package and sends it to Jane. Jane puts a lock on the package as well and sends it back to John. Once John has the package again, he can remove his lock from it and send it back to Jane. When Jane finally gets the package back, only her lock is on it, so she can finally open it up.

52. You don't knock on your own hotel room door.

53. Three candles. Since the others were not extinguished, their wax will melt completely. But the three that were blown out will still be intact.

54. Dr. Canine – he's the better dentist, as he's the only dentist that could have been working on Dr. Molar's teeth.

55. Start both hourglasses as you start boiling the egg. After the seven-minute hourglass runs out, turn it to start it again. Four minutes later, when the eleven-minute hourglass runs out, turn the partially refilled seven-minute hourglass again. Wait for that hourglass to run out, which will take another four minutes and get you to exactly fifteen minutes of boiling time. (But the egg won't be very tasty anymore.)

56. Forty dollars. Break all four links in one of the chains and use those four links to attach the remaining chains together.

57. Take one diamond from the first bag, two from the second, three from the third, four from the fourth, and five from the fifth, and weigh them all together. If the weight on the scale ends in .1, then you know the first bag has the fake diamonds. If the weight on the scale ends in .2, then the second bag has fake diamonds, and so on.

58. About 50:50 (the likelihood of a girl being born is still about 50%).

59. Abby likes to zip-line, Lizzie likes to paint, Stacey likes to hike, and Eliza likes to swim.

60. Milo is hiding under the couch. Luna is getting her ears scratched. Charlie is taking a nap. Leo is eating catnip. Max is playing laser tag.

61. Monday is June's birthday. Tuesday is Sally's birthday. Wednesday is Helga's birthday. Thursday is Pearl's birthday. Friday is May's birthday.

62. Jax, Jerry, James, Jack, John, Jason.

63. Wednesday.

64. Use the shovel to make a pile of dirt below the window and climb out.

65. The break-in was staged. The glass from the broken window was all outside of the house, which means that it had been broken from inside.

66. The Swiss flag is a red flag with a white cross in the center. It can't be hung upside down.

67. He was a lighthouse operator. Turning off the lights caused a shipwreck.

68. The math teacher. He said he was giving a midterm exam, but it was only the first day of school.

69. Nicolas. The abbreviations of the list of chemicals spell out the murderer's name (Ni-C-O-La-S).

70. The man was a firefighter—he caused millions of dollars in damage with the fire hose, but in the process saved hundreds of millions of dollars' worth of art.

71. The water they drank to swallow the pills was poisoned.

72. A snowman.

73. He hid the pocket watch in the freezer in a bag of frozen food. Because of the power failure, the fridge turned off. The neighbor, trying to be helpful, threw out all the spoiled food along with the watch.

74. It was the security guard. He had his name, Michael, on his badge.

75. When he is on the horse, he doesn't count it.

76. The men were in a band, hired to perform at a nightclub.

77. How could someone steal a brooch from behind? It's worn on the front of a shirt.

78. Mark (Question Mark).

79. "Starting" (starting, staring, string, sting, sing, sin, in, I).

80. The parrot was deaf.

81. You can put it on one person's head.

82. Jane takes two other hikers with her. Each hiker begins with a four-day supply of food and water. After the first day, the first hiker gives a one-day supply to Jane and the second hiker, respectively. This leaves the first hiker with a one-day supply to go home, and Jane and the second hiker each have a four-day supply again. After the second day, the second hiker gives Jane a one-day supply and keeps a two-day supply to make it home. This gives Jane a four-day supply of food and water for the final four days of her journey.

83. The professor didn't know who Mary was, so she could slip her exam in the pile and run off, and the professor wouldn't know which exam to penalize.

84. Forty dollars.

85. He counted the pits he'd removed from the plums.

86. The bellhop kept two dollars. The three dollars he gave back, plus the two he kept, equal five dollars; the concierge kept the other twenty-five as the normal payment for the guests' room.

87. It's 5 no matter what.

88. They tilt the barrel until the wine touches the lip. If the bottom of the barrel is visible, it is less than half full. If the bottom of the barrel is still covered, it is more than half full.

89. Three hours. He doesn't have to wait half an hour to take the first pill.

90. No. After driving half a mile, the truck has used up some gas and weighs less.

91. Seventeen dollars and a hot dog.

92. Go to the corner—it's always 90 degrees.

93. He was driving during the daytime.

94. The surgeries were performed so long ago that most of the patients have now died of old age.

95. He divided up the bills in multiples of two: $1, $2, $4, $8, $16, $32, $64, $128, $256, with $489 remaining for the tenth envelope. He can then form any number from 1 to 1,000 from some combination of these amounts.

96. None. The taller person would want to shake hands with a shorter person, but the shorter person wouldn't want to shake hands with the taller person.

97. overburDEN MARKetplaces

98. One—it takes two rabbits to breed.

99. Eleven. Sarah lost three games, so had to win an additional three to break even, and then five more to win the five dollars.

100. Both are wrong—"nothing" and "something" don't rhyme with "orange."

101. Pull out the plug in the bath.

102. Drop it from more than one hundred feet. The vase won't break until it reaches the ground, so if it's more than one hundred feet down, you win!

103. Tina. She names her children after the notes in a scale (Do, Re, Mi, Fa, So, La, Ti, Do).

104. He slid a newspaper under the door, and had Timmy and Tommy stand on each side.

105. Miranda, John, Neville, Jason, Macy.

106. She wrote "The Exact Weight of This Alpaca" instead of a guess.

107. His eyeglasses fell in the sink.